Advent
Meditations
With
Padre Pio

Compiled by Anthony Chiffolo

Liguori

ONE LIGUORI DRIVE
LIGUORI MO 63057-9999

Imprimi Potest:
Thomas D. Picton, C.Ss.R.
Provincial, Denver Province
The Redemptorists

ISBN 978-0-7648-1744-1
© 2008, Liguori Publications
Printed in the United States of America
08 09 10 11 12   5 4 3 2 1

Liguori Publications, a nonprofit corporation, is an apostolate of
the Redemptorists. To learn more about the Redemptorists, visit
Redemptorists.com.

To order, call 800-325-9521
www.liguori.org

*A complete list of the works quoted
in this booklet appears on page 32.*

Introduction

By the time Jesus was born in Bethlehem, the Middle East was in a turmoil of expectation, the people ready for God to do great things on their behalf. During Advent, we commemorate those centuries of Jewish anticipation. The Anointed One for whom we wait, however, is not a warrior-king but an outcast who preached an all-inclusive love, who continues to bring God's blessed community to life each day.

Saint Pio longed to be with the Messiah. One might say Pio's life was a prolonged "advent," a restless anticipation of that blissful moment when he would be with God.

The quotations from Pio's letters allow us to accompany him on his Advent journey. We experience his searching, share his longing, feel his discouragement, and embrace his hope. Perhaps, with God's grace, we may also glimpse his final ecstasy.

Sunday
First Week of Advent

Seeking the Infinite Good

I seem to be searching…for something I cannot find, and….although I don't know what this good is that my heart seeks so badly, I seem to know one thing for certain, that this good is inexhaustible and not circumscribed by limits [and] that my heart will never be able to contain it entirely, for in my ignorance I feel that this is a very great good, an immense good, an infinite good.

Is this Jesus? If not, then who is it?

LETTER TO PADRE AGOSTINO

MAY 6, 1913

"Ask, and it will be given you;
search, and you will find;
knock, and the door will be opened for you."

LUKE 11:9

Monday
First Week of Advent

Desiring to Love

I want to love Jesus as I should. I desire this love; I know I love Him, but—dear God!—how inferior my love is to my desire to love! Ought it not to be the opposite, that my love should surpass the desire for it?

LETTER TO PADRE BENEDETTO

APRIL 7, 1915

*All things work together for good
for those who love God.*

ROMANS 8:28

Tuesday
First Week of Advent

Saying Yes!

Let us pray to the Lord that He may never permit us to shut the ears of our heart to His voice that is speaking to us today.

LETTER TO RAFFAELINA CERASE
JUNE 8, 1915

Then Mary said, "Here am I,
the servant of the Lord;
let it be with me according to your word."

LUKE 1:38

Wednesday
First Week of Advent

Bursting With God-News

Infinite love has at last overcome my hard-heartedness, leaving me weak and powerless. He keeps pouring Himself completely into the small vase of this creature....Because of the exultation of possessing Him in me, I cannot refrain from saying with the most holy Virgin: My spirit rejoices in God my Savior.

LETTER TO PADRE BENEDETTO
JANUARY 12, 1919

"For the Mighty One has done great things for me, and holy is his name."

LUKE 1:49

Thursday
First Week of Advent

Soaring Like Eagles

I have come to the point where I am almost lost in this deep obscurity. Not a glimmer of light, not a moment's respite. I feel my courage failing and the thought that I am going astray…[or] offending God fills me with terror and paralyzes my limbs. Soul and body are pressed down by an enormous weight….The thought of God…still sustains my soul.

LETTER TO PADRE AGOSTINO
SEPTEMBER 4, 1915

Those who wait for the Lord shall renew their strength, they shall mount up with wings like eagles, they shall run and not be weary, they shall walk and not faint.

ISAIAH 40:31

Friday
First Week of Advent

Following Unknown Paths

Now and again a most feeble light penetrates from above, just enough to reassure my poor soul that all is being directed by divine Providence and that through joy and tears the heavenly Father is leading me by inscrutable secret ways to the end He has in view. This is nothing else than the perfection of my soul and its union with God.

LETTER TO PADRE AGOSTINO
JUNE 20, 1915

"I came to bring fire to the earth, and how I wish it were already kindled!"

LUKE 12:49

Saturday
First Week of Advent

Awaiting the Dawn

Blessed are the eyes which will see the dawn of this new day!

LETTER TO PADRE BENEDETTO

MAY 27, 1915

In accordance with his promise,
we wait for new heavens and a new earth.

2 PETER 3:13

Sunday
Second Week of Advent

Hearing the Beloved Voice

In the midst of this deep night of the soul one thing...is left to me: the voice of the one who guides me...Only in this do I [feel]...a slight calm in the midst of so many storms.

LETTER TO PADRE BENEDETTO
DECEMBER 4, 1916

Now there was a great wind, so strong that it was splitting mountains and breaking rocks in pieces before the LORD, but the LORD was not in the wind; and after the wind an earthquake, but the LORD was not in the earthquake; and after the earthquake a fire, but the LORD was not in the fire; and after the fire a sound of sheer silence.

1 KINGS 19:11–12

Monday
Second Week of Advent

Blowing Where the Spirit Wills

We are not all called to the same state and the Holy Spirit doesn't work in all souls in the same way. He "blows as He wills and where He wills."

LETTER TO ANNITA RODOTE
OCTOBER 31, 1915

"The wind blows where it chooses,
and you hear the sound of it,
but you do not know
where it comes from or where it goes.
So it is with everyone
who is born of the Spirit."

JOHN 3:8

Tuesday
Second Week of Advent

Accepting the Divine Gift

In moments of greater spiritual oppression, place yourself in the presence of God and pronounce your *Fiat*! I know that sometimes you will not have the strength to do this, but do not fear. It is essential that you know Jesus is pleased with your spiritual state.

LETTER TO ERMINIA GARGANI

JUNE 28, 1918

"Come, you that are blessed by my Father, inherit the kingdom prepared for you from the foundation of the world."

MATTHEW 25:34

Wednesday
Second Week of Advent

Focusing on the Eternal

Let us fix our gaze constantly on the splendor of the heavenly Jerusalem. Let the consideration of all those good things to be possessed in that realm provide us with delightful food for our thoughts.

LETTER TO RAFFAELINA CERASE

OCTOBER 10, 1914

*"Do not store up for yourselves treasures on
earth, where moth and rust consume and
where thieves break in and steal;
but store up for yourselves treasures in heaven,
where neither moth nor rust consumes
and where thieves do not break in and steal.
For where your treasure is,
there your heart will be also."*

MATTHEW 6:19–21

Thursday
Second Week of Advent

Following My Blessed Mother

We must make every effort, like many elect souls, to follow invariably this Blessed Mother, to walk close to her since there is no other path leading to life except the path followed by our Mother. Let us not refuse to take this path, we who want to reach our journey's end.

LETTER TO PADRE AGOSTINO

JULY 1, 1915

She is a reflection of eternal light,
a spotless mirror of the working of God,
and an image of his goodness.

WISDOM OF SOLOMON 7:26

Friday
Second Week of Advent

Heeding My Good Shepherd

To be afraid of being lost in the arms of divine Goodness is more peculiar than the fear of a baby held tightly in the arms of its mother.

LETTER TO ANNITA RODOTE

AUGUST 16, 1918

"I am the good shepherd. I know my own and my own know me, just as the Father knows me and I know the Father. And I lay down my life for the sheep."

JOHN 10:14–15

Saturday
Second Week of Advent

Keeping On

If it seems to you that you always desire without ever arriving at the possession of perfect love, all this means that your soul must never say it has enough, it means that we cannot and must not stop on the path to divine love and holy perfection.

LETTER TO RAFFAELINA CERASE
APRIL 20, 1915

Now I know only in part; then I will know fully, even as I have been fully known.

1 CORINTHIANS 13:12

Sunday
Third Week of Advent

Looking Within

Don't make any effort to look for God outside yourself, because He is there within you; He is with you, in your weeping and in your seeking.

LETTER TO PADRE BENEDETTO

JANUARY 30, 1921

"I saw the Lord always before me,
for he is at my right hand
so that I will not be shaken."

ACTS 2:25

Monday
Third Week of Advent

Praying Simply

Let this beautiful exclamation always be in your heart and on your lips throughout all the events of your life. Say it in times of affliction; say it in times of temptation….Say it again when you feel yourself submerged in the ocean of love for Jesus; it will be your anchor and salvation.

LETTER TO ANNITA RODOTE

FEBRUARY 6, 1915

"Your kingdom come. Your will be done, on earth as it is in heaven."

MATTHEW 6:10

Tuesday
Third Week of Advent

Having God-Strength

You must have boundless faith in the divine goodness, for the victory is absolutely certain. How could you think otherwise? Isn't our God more concerned about our salvation than we are ourselves? Isn't He stronger than hell itself? Who can ever resist and overcome the King of the heavens? What are the world, the devil, the flesh and all our enemies before the Lord?

LETTER TO RAFFAELINA CERASE
APRIL 25, 1914

*"It is the LORD your God who goes with you,
to fight for you against your enemies,
to give you victory."*

DEUTERONOMY 20:4

Wednesday
Third Week of Advent

Watching for Signs

You are suffering and are right to complain. By all means complain and in a loud voice, but fear nothing. The victim of Love is impatient to possess it; it must cry out that it can take no more and that it is impossible to resist the treatment of the Beloved who wants her and leaves her, and leaves her while he wants her.

LETTER TO MARIA GARGANI

APRIL 28, 1919

*Therefore the Lord himself will give you
a sign. Look, the young woman is
with child and shall bear a son,
and shall name him Immanuel.*

ISAIAH 7:14

Thursday
Third Week of Advent

Praying Confidently

It is true that God's power triumphs over everything: but humble and suffering prayer triumphs over God Himself!

LETTER TO ANNITA RODOTE

AUGUST 27, 1915

Return to the LORD, your God,
for he is gracious and merciful, slow to anger,
and abounding in steadfast love,
and relents from punishing.

JOEL 2:13

Friday
Third Week of Advent

Pursuing God's Way to Heaven

Why should the soul…worry whether it reaches the Homeland by way of the desert or through fields?! As long as God is with you always…why should the poor soul be afflicted?!…Submit yourself to His…will and do not believe you would serve Him better in a different state, because one only serves Him well when one serves Him as he wishes.

LETTER TO MARIA GARGANI
NOVEMBER 4, 1916

"Naked I came from my mother's womb, and naked shall I return there; the LORD gave, and the LORD has taken away; blessed be the name of the LORD."

JOB 1:21

Saturday
Third Week of Advent

Giving Thanks Along the Way

You ought to ask Our Lord for just one thing: to love Him. All the rest should be thanksgiving.

LETTER TO PADRE BENEDETTO
NOVEMBER 20, 1921

Rejoice always, pray without ceasing,
give thanks in all circumstances;
for this is the will of God
in Christ Jesus for you.

1 THESSALONIANS 5:16–18

Sunday
Fourth Week of Advent

Thirsting for Living Water

Do you want great love from me, Jesus? I too desire this, just as a deer longs to reach a flowing stream, but as you see I have no more love to give! Give me some more and I'll offer it to you!

LETTER TO RAFFAELINA CERASE
APRIL 20, 1915

As a deer longs for flowing streams,
so my soul longs for you, O God.
My soul thirsts for God,
for the living God.
When shall I come and behold
the face of God?

PSALM 42:1–2

Monday
Fourth Week of Advent

Straining to "See"

I keep my eyes fixed on the East...to discover that miraculous star which guided our forebears to the Grotto of Bethlehem.... The more I fix my gaze the dimmer my sight becomes;...the more ardent my search, the deeper the darkness which envelops me. I am alone by day and by night and no ray of light comes through to enlighten me.

LETTER TO PADRE BENEDETTO

MARCH 8, 1916

"The kingdom of God is not coming with things that can be observed; nor will they say, 'Look, here it is!' or 'There it is!' For, in fact, the kingdom of God is among you."

LUKE 17:20–21

Tuesday
Fourth Week of Advent

Believing Against the Evidence

God is not present where there is not a desire to love Him.

LETTER TO THE VENTRELLA SISTERS

DECEMBER 15, 1916

"Have you believed because you have seen me? Blessed are those who have not seen and yet have come to believe."

JOHN 20:29

Wednesday
Fourth Week of Advent

Accepting God's Giving

We must have great confidence in divine Providence in order to practice holy simplicity….we must imitate the people of God when they were in the desert. These people were severely forbidden to gather more manna than they needed for one day….Do not doubt…that God will provide for the next day, and all the days of our pilgrimage.

LETTER TO ERMINIA GARGANI

MARCH 3, 1917

"Do not worry about your life,
what you will eat, or about your body,
what you will wear. For life is more than food,
and the body more than clothing."

LUKE 12:22–23

Thursday
Fourth Week of Advent

Sailing Toward God

[Do not] worry about your own soul. Jesus loves you all the time…[so]what is there to fear? Be careful…not to let your occupations…cause you anxiety, and although you set out over the waves and against the wind of many perplexities,…say to Our Lord continually: "Dear God, I am rowing and sailing for you; be my pilot and my oarsman yourself."

LETTER TO PADRE AGOSTINO
NOVEMBER 19, 1916

"God has granted safety to all those who are sailing with you." So keep up your courage, men, for I have faith in God that it will be exactly as I have been told.

ACTS 27:24–25

Friday
Fourth Week of Advent

Yearning With Confidence

You know well that perfect love is acquired when one possesses the object of this love, which is God himself. But God will not be possessed totally and perfectly except in the Homeland; not while we are in exile.... Therefore, if this is our state, why so much frenzied anxiety and useless dejection? Yearn and yearn always, but see that it is with greater confidence, and without any fear.

LETTER TO ERMINIA GARGANI

APRIL 11, 1918

For I know that my Redeemer lives, and that at the last he will stand upon the earth.

JOB 19:25

Saturday
Fourth Week of Advent

Drowning in the Infinite

I am drowned in the immense ocean of the love of my Beloved.…It is true that it is inside and outside me. But, dear God, when you pour yourself into the little vase of my being I… [cannot] contain you. The inner walls of this heart feel…about to burst.…When the whole of this love is unable to enter such a little vase, it flows over onto the outside. How can one contain the Infinite in oneself?

LETTER TO PADRE BENEDETTO
JANUARY 29, 1919

Many waters cannot quench love, neither can floods drown it. If one offered for love all the wealth of one's house, it would be…scorned.

SONG OF SOLOMON 8:7

Sources

Padre Pio of Pietrelcina. *Letters: Volume I:
Correspondence with His Spiritual Directors
(1910–1922)*. Edited by Melchiorre of Pobladura
and Alessandro of Ripabottoni. English version
edited by Father Gerardo Di Flumeri, O.F.M. Cap.
San Giovanni Rotondo (Foggia), Italy: Our Lady
of Grace Capuchin Friary, 1984.

Padre Pio of Pietrelcina. *Letters: Volume II: Correspondence with Raffaelina Cerase, Noblewoman
(1914–1915)*. Edited by Melchiorre of Pobladura
and Alessandro of Ripabottoni. English version
edited by Father Gerardo Di Flumeri, O.F.M. Cap.
San Giovanni Rotondo (Foggia), Italy: Our Lady
of Grace Capuchin Friary, 1997.

Padre Pio of Pietrelcina. *Letters: Volume III:
Correspondence with His Spiritual Daughters
(1915–1923)*. Edited by Melchiorre of Pobladura
and Alessandro of Ripabottoni. English version
edited by Father Alessio Parente, O.F.M. Cap. San
Giovanni Rotondo (Foggia), Italy: Our Lady of
Grace Capuchin Friary, 1994.